A FIRST LOOK AT BIRDS

A FIRST LOOK AT BIRDS

By Millicent E. Selsam and Joyce Hunt

ILLUSTRATED BY HARRIETT SPRINGER

WALKER AND COMPANY
NEW YORK

To Irwin, our favorite odd bird

The authors wish to thank Robert
Arbib, Editor of *American Birds,* for
reading the text of this book.

Text copyright © 1973 by Millicent E. Selsam and Joyce Hunt
Illustrations copyright © 1973 by Harriett Springer

First published in the United States of America
in 1973 by the Walker Publishing Company, Inc.

Published simultaneously in Canada by Fitzhenry & Whiteside, Limited, Toronto.

Trade ISBN: 0-8027-6163-1
Reinf. ISBN: 0-8027-6164-X

Library of Congress Catalog Card Number: 73-81404

Printed in the United States of America.

10 9 8 7 6 5 4 3 2 1

A FIRST LOOK AT SERIES

Each of the nature books for this series is planned to develop the child's powers of observation.

What is a bird?

A bird is an animal that almost always flies.

This is an animal that flies.
Is it a bird?

No, it is a bumblebee.

This is another animal that flies.
Is it a bird?

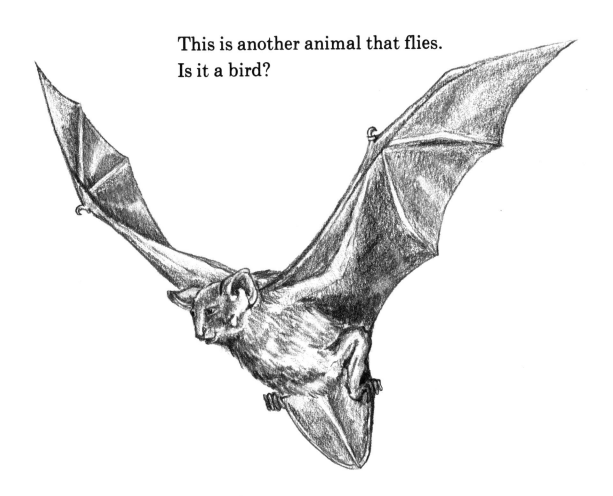

No, it is a bat.

This is still another animal that flies.
Is it a bird?

HERRING GULL

Yes, it is a bird because it has feathers.
No other animal has feathers.

This is an animal that does not fly.
Is it a bird?

PENGUIN

If it has feathers, it is a bird even though it cannot fly.

Not all birds look alike.
They may have parts that have different shapes.

BARN OWL

WHISTLING SWAN

Find the bird with a long neck.

Find the bird that looks as if it has no neck.

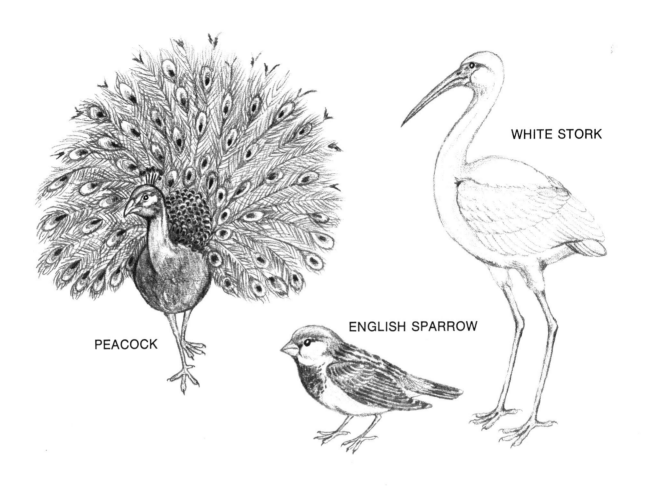

WHITE STORK

PEACOCK

ENGLISH SPARROW

Find the bird that looks as if it is standing on two sticks.

Find the bird with a fan of feathers.

Find the bird that looks like the ones you see in the park.

Birds may have different bills (or beaks).

SPOONBILL

SWORD-BILLED
HUMMINGBIRD

Find the bill that looks like a straight sword.

Find the bill that is shaped like a spoon.

RED CROSSBILL

FLAMINGO

LONG-BILLED CURLEW

Find the bill that looks like a curved sword.

Find the bird whose bill looks like a broken nose.

Find the bird whose bill is crossed at the tips.

15

But most birds do not have such fancy bills.

Find the short, thin, pointed bill.
Find the short, thick, cone-shaped bill.
Find the long, pointed bill.
Find the hooked bill.

The shape of the bill helps the bird catch and eat
its special kind of food.
Birds use their bills as we use a knife, fork, and spoon.

Birds with short, pointed bills usually pick up or dig out insects.

Birds with short, thick, cone-shaped bills usually crack open seeds.

Birds with hooked bills usually tear the flesh of small animals.

Birds with long, pointed bills usually spear fish or frogs.

CHICKADEE

GOLDFINCH

OSPREY

TERN

You can tell birds apart by their color.

The cardinal is almost all red.

The scarlet tanager is red with black wings and a black tail.

The red-winged blackbird is black with a patch of red on its wings.

CARDINAL

SCARLET TANAGER

RED-WINGED BLACKBIRD

19

The indigo bunting is blue all over.

The bluejay is blue, black, and white.

Which is which?

You can find yellow, green, purple, orange, and many other colors in birds.

Sometimes it is hard to tell one bird from another
by its bill or its color.
But you can tell by its size.
A hawk and an eagle look very much alike.
How can you tell them apart?
The hawk is usually a smaller bird.

21

A goose is bigger than a duck.

Which is which?

Most birds have three or four toes.
Find the toes that are webbed.

Find the foot with two toes in front and two behind.

Find the foot with three toes in front and one short
toe behind.

Find the foot with three toes in front and one long
toe behind.

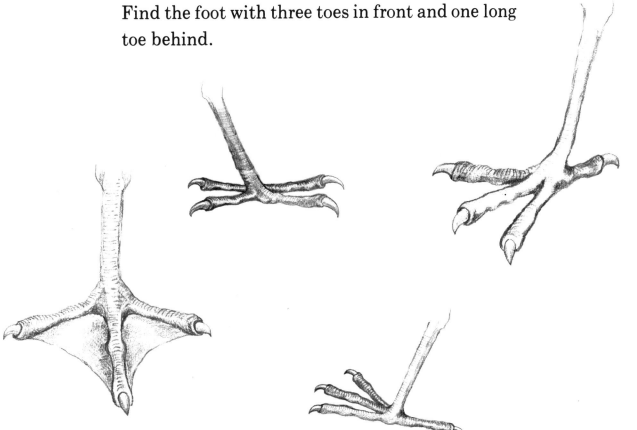

Ducks swim. Birds that swim usually have webbed feet.

Woodpeckers climb. Many birds that climb have feet with two toes in front and two toes behind.

Chickens walk. Many birds that walk have three toes in front and one short toe behind.

Robins perch. Birds that perch have three toes in front and one long toe behind that helps them clamp onto a branch.

A Puzzle:

Which feet go on which bird?

CHICKEN

WOODPECKER

DUCK

ROBIN

You can tell certain birds by the way they fly.

Cranes fly with their necks stretched out in front.

Herons fly with their necks tucked in an S curve.

Which is which?

26

The bald eagle flies with its wings held straight out.

The vulture flies with its wings held up in the form of a V.

Which is which?

Some birds have feathers in funny places.
Some birds have no feathers in funny places.

Find the bird that looks as if it has a moustache.

Find the bird that looks as if it is wearing a hat.

Find the bird that has a naked head.

VULTURE

FROGMOUTH

VICTORIA CROWNED PIGEON

29

Birds may have streaks (or stripes) in different places.

Find the bird with a streaked head.

Find the bird with the streaked breast.

BROWN THRASHER

WORM-EATING WARBLER

Sometimes you have to look closely to tell two birds apart.

The song sparrow has a black spot on its breast but so does the tree sparrow.

Which is which?

The song sparrow has streaks on its breast.

The tree sparrow does not.

When you look at a bird you have to notice many things.

Look at the shape.

Look at the bill.

Look at the size.

Look at the feet.

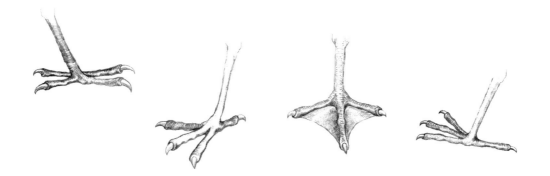

Look at the way it flies.

Look for feathers (or no feathers) in funny places.

Look at streaks.

And don't forget—look at the color, too